No portion of this book may be reproduced in any form without the expressed written consent of the author or publisher. All rights reserved.
Printed in the United States of America

# What is the Box

© 2017 by Denniz Cargile
ISBN 978-0-9967111-3-5
First Edition
2 4 6 8 10 9 7 5 3 1

Cover design and layout by Jeffrey L. Davidson
Book design by Jeffrey L. Davidson and Denniz Cargile
Interior illustrations by Jeffrey L. Davidson

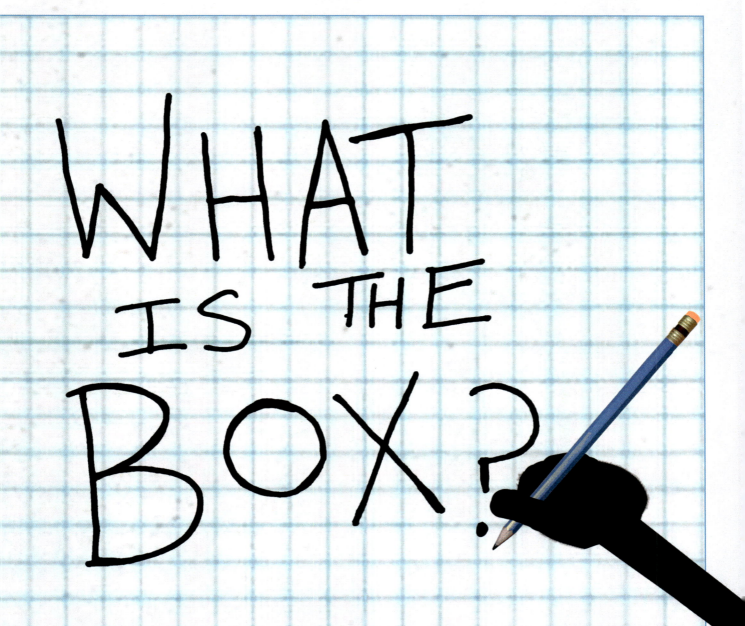

# WHAT IS THE BOX?

Words by Denniz Cargile
Art by Jeffrey L. Davidson

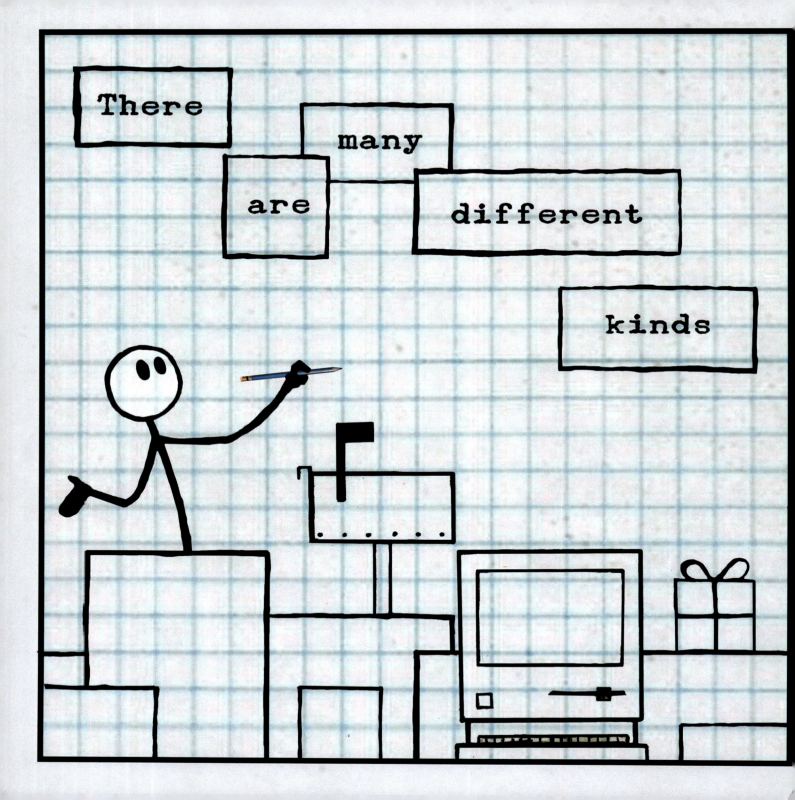

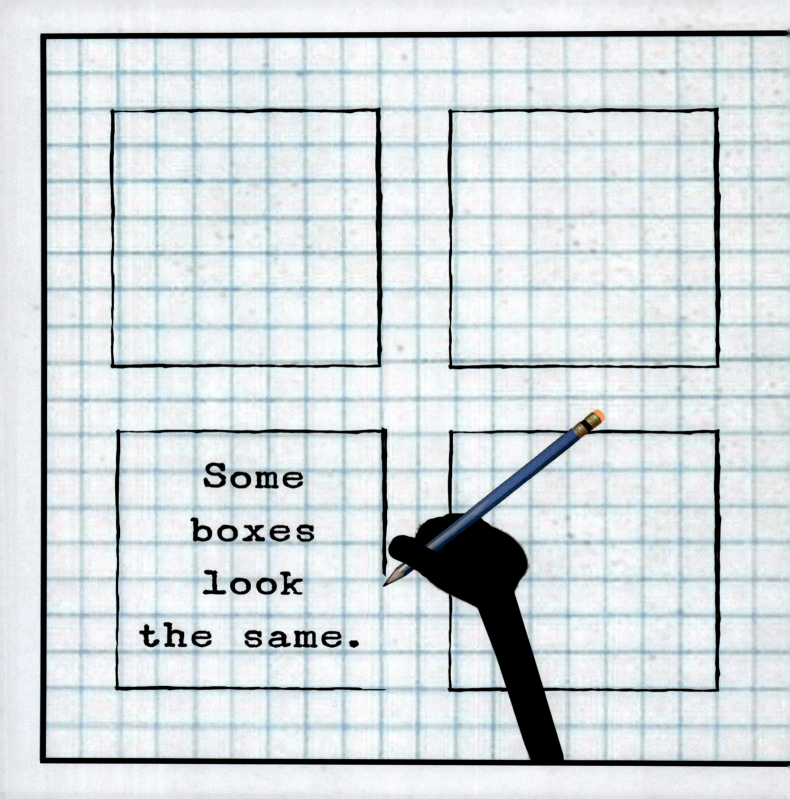

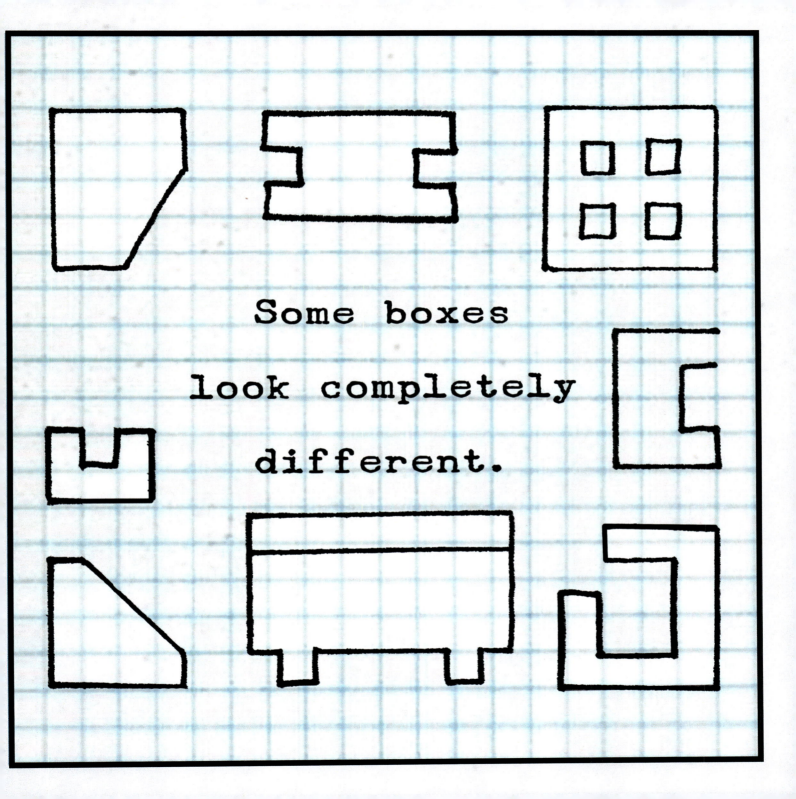

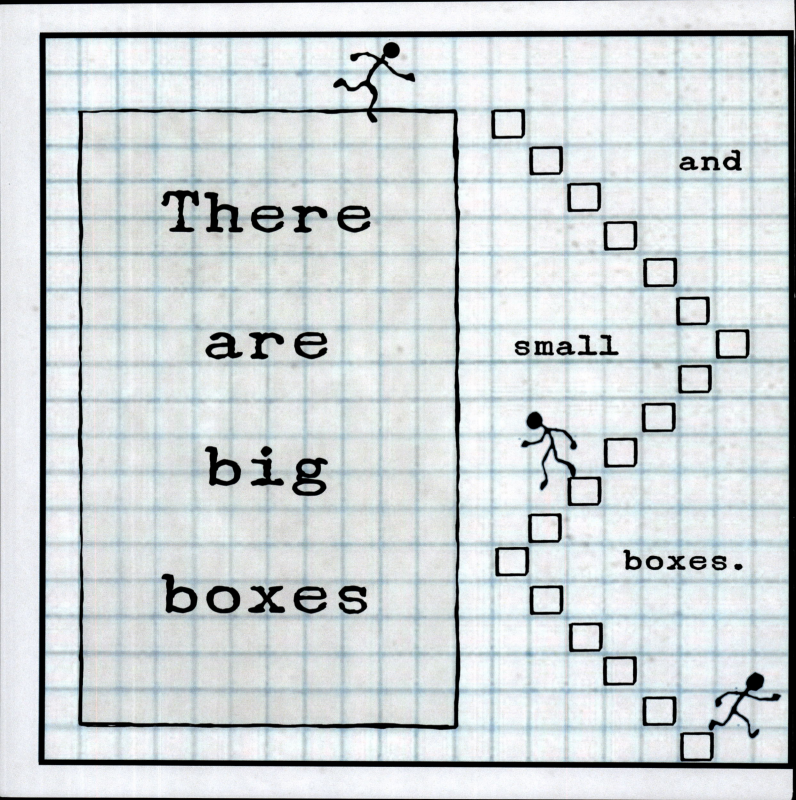

Strong boxes

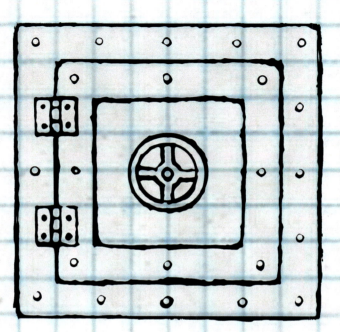

and weak boxes.

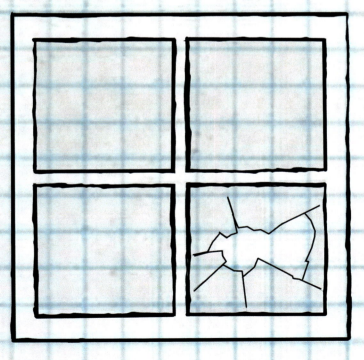

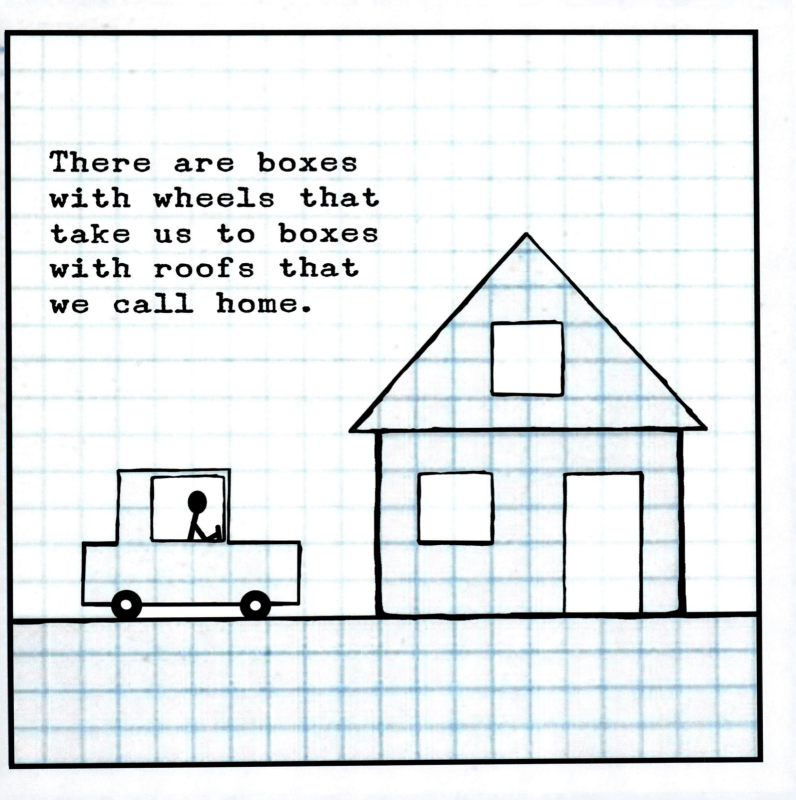

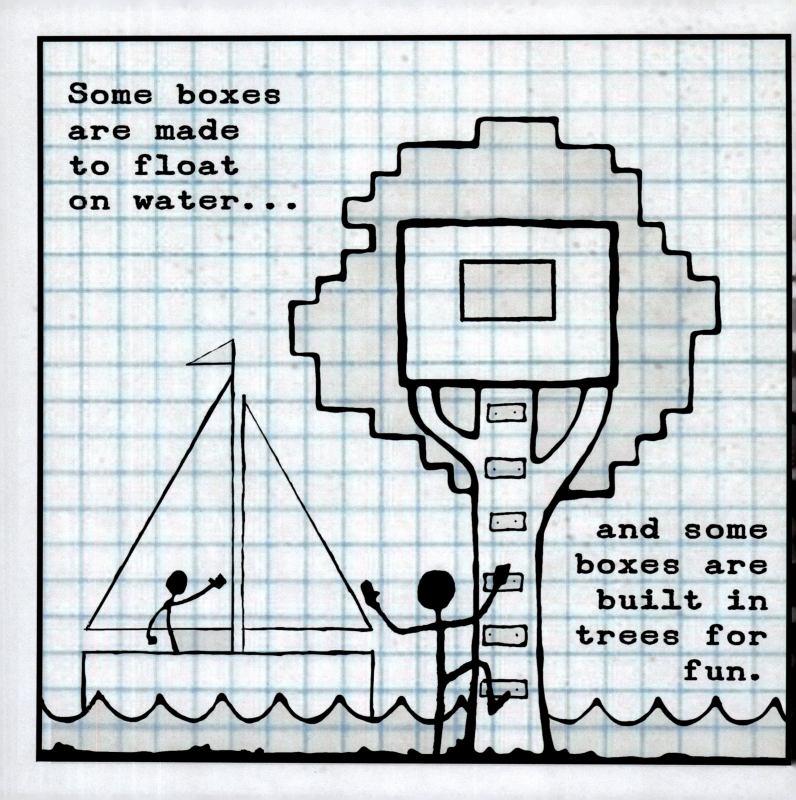

...some boxes even have bars.

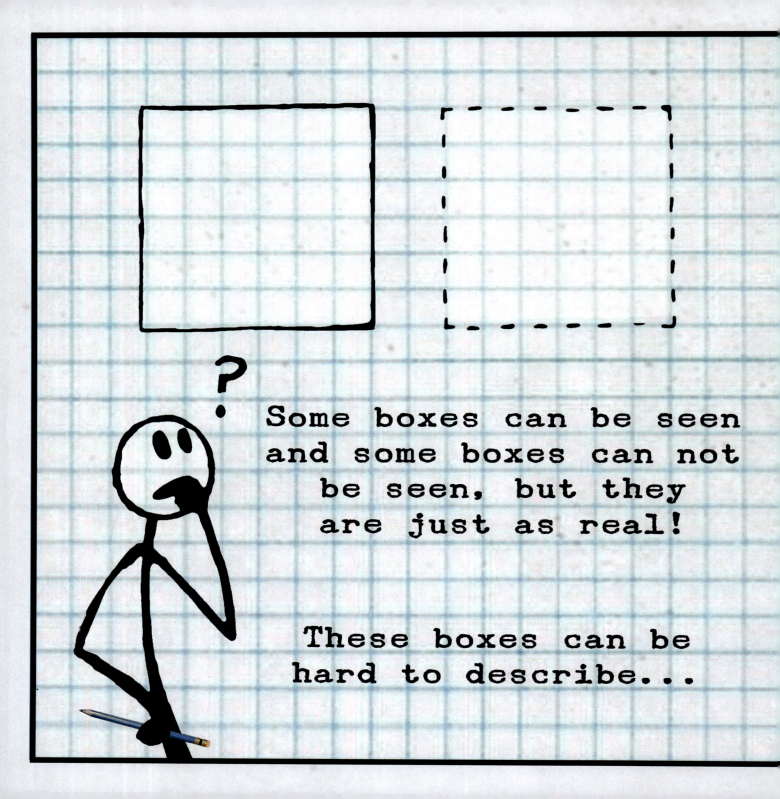

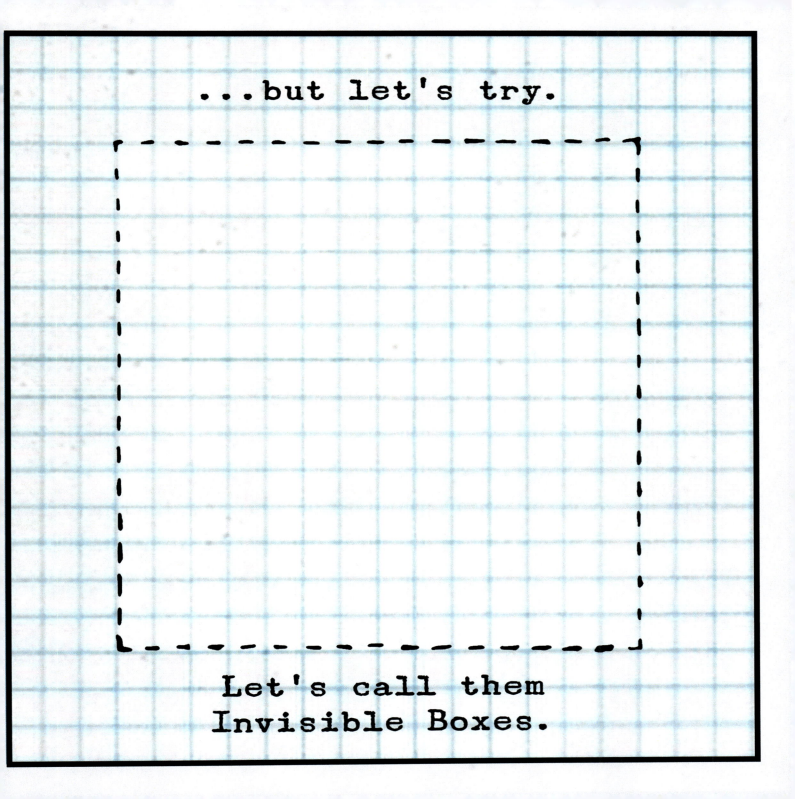

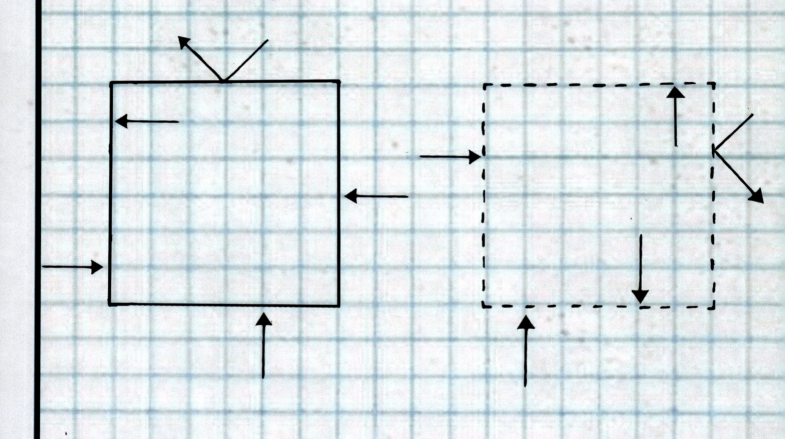

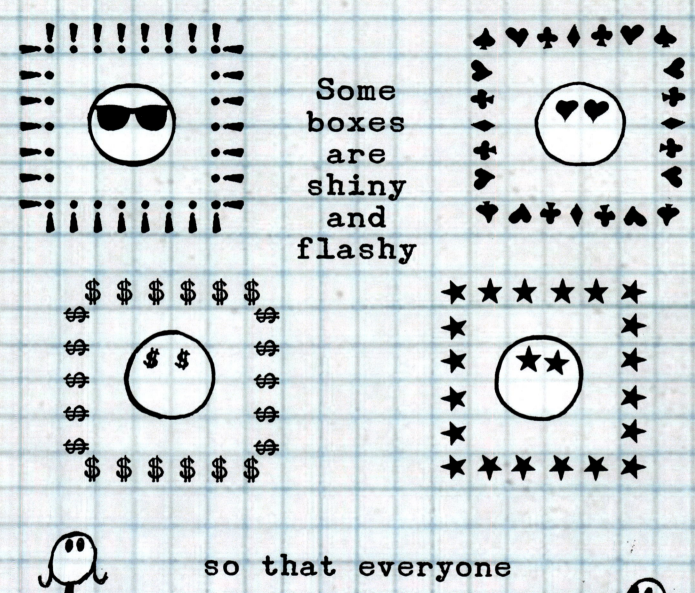

Some make angry boxes to keep others from hurting them.

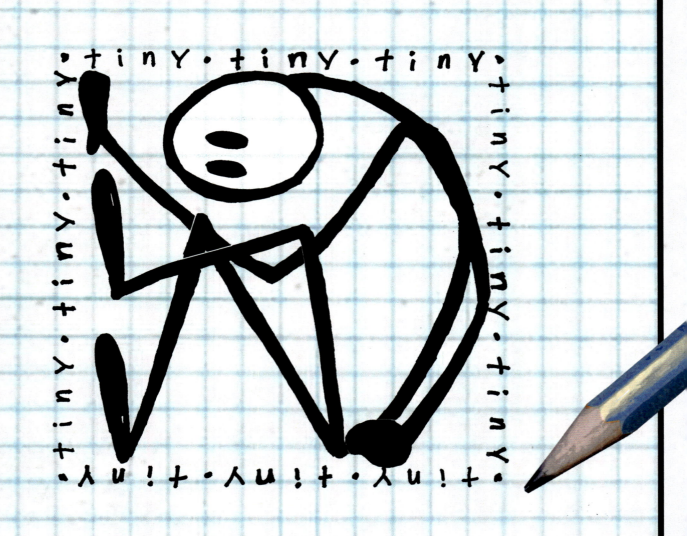

...but if tried hard enough even GIANTS can fit into tiny boxes.

There are...

sad boxes,

fun boxes,

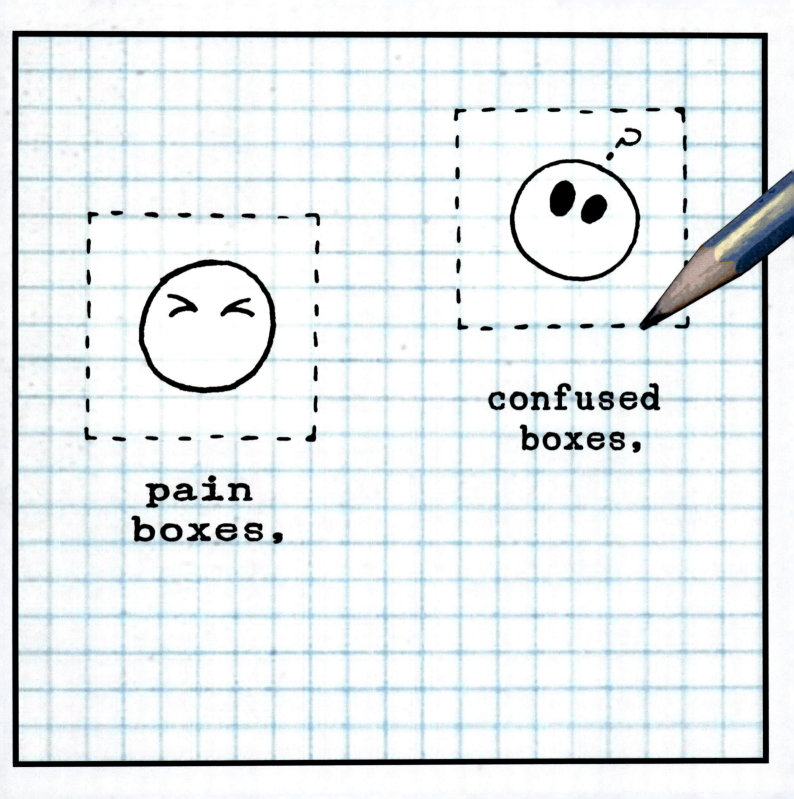

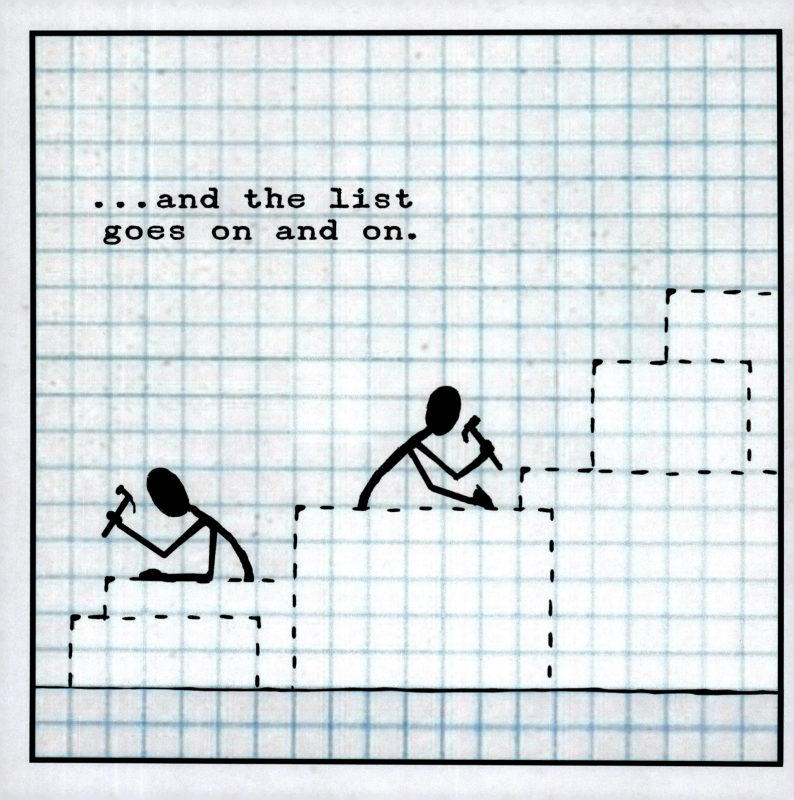

You might have to squeeze a bit ...

push a pinch ...

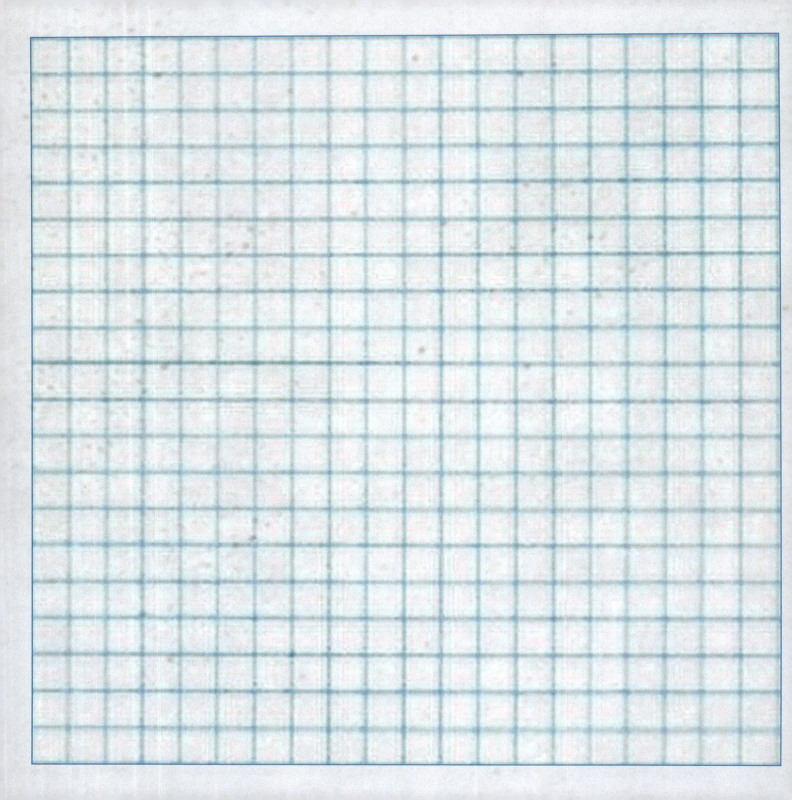

Made in the USA
Monee, IL
25 October 2023